GOD *is* GOOD & JUST

K.C. Thrall
Illustrated by Alexis Bales

WestBow Press books may be ordered through booksellers or by contacting:

WestBow Press
A Division of Thomas Nelson & Zondervan
1663 Liberty Drive
Bloomington, IN 47403
www.westbowpress.com
844-714-3454

Interior Image Credit: Alexis Bales

ISBN: 978-1-6642-4648-5 (sc)
ISBN: 978-1-6642-4650-8 (hc)
ISBN: 978-1-6642-4649-2 (e)

Library of Congress Control Number: 2021921112

Print information available on the last page.

WestBow Press rev. date: 11/10/2021

WESTBOW
PRESS®
A DIVISION OF THOMAS NELSON
& ZONDERVAN

Dedicated to:

My husband, Tyson, for blessing me with the opportunity to embrace God's goodness. You are my "iron sharpening iron," and I wouldn't have it any other way.

I am proud to be your wife.

My beloved son, Titus, in whom I delight. I pray you grow to be a man after God's own heart.

My beautiful niece, Lucy, the first child to ever capture my heart. Always remember that you are "far more precious than jewels."

I love each of you endlessly.

God is good and just.
Oh, it's really true!

God is good and just; more
fair than me or you.

You may not understand His ways,

you may not think them right.

But trust His plan and understand
He makes everything upright.

God is good and just, a hard balance that we can't find.

God's justice is not slow,
but perfectly in time.

His grace is so abundant!

His forgiveness
is so pure!

We can trust His rulings
and know He is our cure.

So, don't be mad, sad or bad but trust and see firsthand...

God's ways are good, right and true!
His ways will always stand.

"God loves whatever is just and good; the unfailing love of the Lord fills the earth." Psalm 33:5

Printed in the United States
by Baker & Taylor Publisher Services